CALM

CALM

Interiors to
nurture, relax
and restore

SALLY DENNING
photography by Polly Wreford

RYLAND PETERS & SMALL
LONDON • NEW YORK

To my boys, Freddie and Billy.

SENIOR DESIGNER Megan Smith
SENIOR COMMISSIONING EDITOR
Annabel Morgan
LOCATION RESEARCH Jess Walton
HEAD OF PRODUCTION
Patricia Harrington
ART DIRECTOR Leslie Harrington
PUBLISHER Cindy Richards

First published in 2021 by
Ryland Peters & Small
20–21 Jockey's Fields
London WC1R 4BW
and
341 E 116th Street
New York, NY 10029

www.rylandpeters.com

10 9 8 7 6 5 4 3 2

ISBN 978-1-78879-383-4

A CIP record for this book is available
from the British Library.

Library of Congress CIP data has been
applied for.

Printed and bound in China

MIX
Paper from
responsible sources
FSC® C106563
FSC
www.fsc.org

CONTENTS

WELCOME

I've lost count of the number of different homes I've worked in during my many years as an interior stylist and art director, but the thing that always leaves an impact is the way they make me feel. There are places I can't wait to leave, others that I love but am happy to leave after a shoot, and a few where I would be more than happy to move straight in and stay forever. These tend to be filled with texture or muted colour, are rich in natural elements such as wood or stone and have interesting features, considered corners and pleasing vignettes that fire my imagination and pull at my heartstrings. Put simply, our physical surroundings have a direct correlation with the way that we feel and make an important contribution to our emotional well-being.

The place we call home has always been a backdrop to a variety of activities, but at the time of writing most of us have probably spent more time there than ever before. Home is now a place where we live, work, sleep, eat, exercise, love and laugh, and, hopefully, where we can be ourselves, kick back, gather with friends and family and recharge. It is so important that this place works well for us and offers a sense of retreat and escape – a sanctuary, a safe place. Creating a home that exudes a powerful sense of calm is beneficial on every level, protecting us from the outside world and allowing us to flourish and feel nurtured and secure.

The aim of this book is to provide ideas, tips and tricks for creating a restful, restorative space that makes your shoulders drop the moment you walk through the door. First, I describe the essential foundations of a comforting environment: calming and harmonious colour; lots of appealing textures; an abundance of textiles; quiet pattern and calming decorative details such as plants, flowers and other natural elements. I go on to explore 12 different homes that all have one thing in common: a timeless, tranquil atmosphere that is a pleasure to come home to. I hope this book delivers a sense of peace on each and every page, encouraging you to pause, be present and take a breath – something that we all need more than ever.

STRESS BUSTERS
The muted blue tones of this Georgian living room instil an immediate sense of tranquillity, thanks to the colour choice and easy-on-the-eye furniture and accessories (*opposite*). Getting our dog Buster has changed family life for the better; he's a constant source of happiness and the most wonderful stress reliever. This is Henry the beagle, who you'll also see further on in the book (*above*).

CREATING A
SENSE OF CALM

CALMING
COLOURS

Creating a restful space that makes your shoulders drop the moment you walk through the door can be achieved in many ways, and getting the colour palette right is one of them. Colours can stimulate and excite, but they can also make us feel relaxed and at peace – just what you want in a calm home.

NATURAL INSPIRATION
I'm lucky enough to work with colour almost every day in my job as an interior stylist and draw most of my inspiration from nature, where colours harmonize together beautifully and instinctively. Different natural tones have different connotations. Restful tones include green, associated with peace and calm (*above right and opposite*), and pink, believed to reduce aggression (*above centre*), while earthy browns signal safety and security (*above left*).

OFF-WHITES
& NEUTRALS

Neutral hues, ranging from off-whites to earthy clay and tobacco shades, are known for their calming qualities. They have an association with the natural landscape – sand, rocks and soil – and provide the eye with a restful alternative to brighter colours. Gentle, sludgy neutrals are versatile, working well in all parts of the home, and will add a sense of warmth and sophistication to any scheme. They have the ability to enhance a space, making walls appear to recede and ceilings feel higher, which in turn creates a sense of airy tranquillity. I've always been a fan, mostly using off-whites and neutrals as a useful blank canvas to which I can add or subtract colour as desired. To my mind, they are never cold, never dated and never boring, especially if you add oodles of delicious different textures to keep the space interesting. Classic and timeless, these shades will work hard to make any room fresh and serene.

THE BRIGHT SIDE

Production of the hormone serotonin, responsible for feelings of happiness and well-being, is stimulated by exposure to bright light, so light-filled rooms can elevate our mood and help us feel calmer and more focused. Reducing visual noise and keeping living spaces pared down and uncluttered will also foster a tranquil feel. In these schemes, the addition of rich wood, tactile washed linens, chunky ceramics and simple lighting brings interest and depth to white walls without distracting from the sense of airiness in the room (*this page and opposite*).

DELICATE PASTELS

In colour theory, adding white to any colour results in a tint, and the more you add, the paler the tint will become. Pastels are tinted colours. less saturated in purity and intensity of colour than other colours, so they inspire a fresh, soothing and peaceful vibe in the home. They are the kindest, softest tones in the colour wheel, so tend to be associated with spring and feelings of rebirth and new beginnings. Rooms painted in these shades feel inviting, cosy and soothing, and they are often chosen for bedrooms, bathrooms and children's rooms for this reason, but they can work anywhere. Pastels come into their own when teamed with a natural element like stone or wood, which prevents them from feeling childlike or sugary. When teamed with darker tones such as black, earthy brown or charcoal grey, pastels feel grounded and take on a more interesting or even contemporary edge.

SOFT INSPIRATIONS

Quiet pastel hues are soothing and comfortable to live with (*this page and opposite*). Adding contemporary touches in the form of interesting accessories or accent paint colours sharpens the effect. Monochrome frames give pale pink a grown-up quality (*opposite*), while a deep forest green on the woodwork/trim prevents a pale grey interior from looking bland (*above right*).

MUTED TONES

These wonderful hues are soothing, tranquil tones that you almost want to reach out and touch or stroke. They are are created when a colour is desaturated with black, grey or a complementary colour, resulting in a subtle shade that's easy on the eye. Muted tones speak softly and quietly rather than shouting out, 'Hey, look at me!'. They are the opposite of vivid colours that pop; instead, they calm and ground a space with their knocked-back colour. Any colour can be muted, from pink to yellow to blue, and any muted tone will help to create a reposeful, quiet scheme; all you need do is choose the intensity (or depth of colour) that is desired. Sticking to muted tones throughout an entire home will ensure that the decor works well as a whole, creating a smooth, calm visual pathway from one room to the next rather than jumping about in a mismatched manner.

SUBTLE HINTS

Muted colours bring a calming quality to any room. Soft green sits restfully behind chunky wooden shelves and piles of white ceramics, adding a sense of warmth and earthiness to this Welsh farmhouse kitchen (*above*). A deep neutral browny-pink shade tones beautifully with ikebana floristry (*opposite*). These subtle, muted colours help your eyes to rest in a busy world.

BOLDER
COLOUR

Darker tones have lots of character and will introduce a sense of drama and personality to any room, whether in a modern or period home. Very rich hues have an almost bottomless depth that the eye can find hard to focus on, so a wall painted in such a colour may appear further away than it really is. This can also be the case if the whole room – walls, ceiling and woodwork/trim – is painted in the same tone; it's a bold approach that creates an enveloping, cocooning feel that's very calming. Opting to paint a room one single colour in this way can also make it feel bigger, as the colour flows uninterrupted across every feature. Colours that hark back to the natural world are the best choices here: blues and greens reminiscent of the sky, sea and plants are restful and will work in any room. Dark neutrals are soothing and relaxing too; shades ranging from aubergine/eggplant to chocolate and deep taupe will exude tranquillity in any interior.

DRAMATIC BACKDROPS

Bold, saturated colours create richness, warmth and interest. Adding wooden wall panelling, as seen here in a pinky-red bathroom and green bedroom, introduces extra texture and contrast to a scheme, especially when the light hits it (*opposite and above right*). Painting the whole interior in a single strong colour will bring an enveloping feel of comfort and security (*above left*).

CALMING
TEXTURES

For me, a home without texture is a home without soul, and it's one of the key design elements you must include when decorating. Maybe it's the beautiful patina of old wood or weather-worn brick that puts you at ease, sparking an association with the outdoors and the elements, or perhaps the gentle softness of well-washed linen fabric makes you want to reach out and touch it.

LAYERING TEXTURE
Colour works hard to bring interest to an interior, but it's natural elements like stone, wood, hessian, linen and raw brick that give it an organic, multilayered feel which, in my view, can't be beaten. Untreated elements like the ones shown here work well in any scheme – bare stone, unpainted wood and organic linen will soften a space, giving it the feeling that it's always been there, even in a newly built home (*this page*). Mixing bare brickwork and stripped wood with sleek, modern cabinets in this kitchen adds a calming tactility and timeless quality (*opposite*).

WALLS

Walls are the biggest area within a room, so adding or revealing texture here will immediately make your space feel more tactile and inviting. There are several ways to add textural interest. Using naturally pigmented paints with a chalky, living finish (such as those by Edward Bulmer) will give you a velvety depth of colour, while a lime paint (try Bauwerk) will create a soft wash of colour that you want to stroke. Painting walls, ceilings and architectural details all the same shade means no visual breaks to distract the eye, which brings a great sense of calm. Painted wooden panelling or cladding is another brilliant way to add interest, and can be found in DIY/hardware stores. Painted or raw brick, exposed stone, wooden cladding or reclaimed timber panelling are an integral part of creating a scheme that feels peaceful and relaxed.

WONDER WALLS

Whatever the finish on the walls, keep it simple and fuss free. Lime plaster slurry over stone retains texture and interest yet keeps this room light and bright (*opposite*); Clayworks breathable plaster has a soft, chalky, tactile feel (*this page*). A stone wall and brick fire surround has a timeless quality, while wall tiles play with light and shade, creating an impression of gentle movement (*pages 24 and 25*).

FLOORS

Floors are usually the second-largest area within a room, so the finish is key to how it will look, feel and sound. Opting for textural flooring will add visual and tactile interest; consider natural floorcoverings such as sisal, jute and coir, which are versatile and hard-wearing. The softest and most tactile option is, of course, carpet; it feels luxurious underfoot and is ideal for dulling noise. Quarried stone, such as limestone and slate flagstones, will bring a grounded earthiness to a room, while reclaimed floorboards add a pleasing patina, and both options work well with underfloor heating for a gentle radiant warmth. Old floorboards look wonderful sanded and sealed; alternatively you can paint them using floor paint for a totally bespoke look. Layer up with rugs to add interest, pattern or colour, but do mix in some plains, as bold pattern can easily dominate and make a calm scheme feel unbalanced.

FLOOR SHOW
Microcement on a landing/upstairs hallway gives the illusion of softness underfoot, despite its tough, durable finish. The soft grey colour tones with the wall colour so that the two are in harmony rather than competing for attention (*this page*). The painstaking placement of pamment tiles cut from reclaimed 19th-century bricks from Eastern Europe not only looks pleasing but brings subtle texture to this uncluttered hallway (*opposite*).

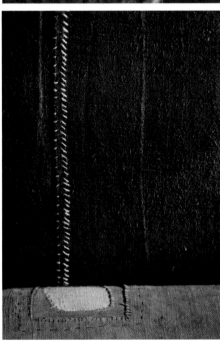

TEXTILES

Touch is key. A hug from a friend or loved one can instantly bring peace and serenity, and filling your home with inviting and tactile textiles will have the same effect.

As a stylist, I think textiles are probably the quickest way to create a relaxed, easy-going look, and they are a firm favourite in my home. There are options to suit all different homes and lifestyles – choose loose-weave washed linen and sturdy practical cotton plains or ticking if you have children or pets and anticipate that items will be in and out of the washing machine. More luxurious, tactile choices include sheepskin, natural wool, luscious velvet or chunky cord and bobbly bouclé, and don't forget that natural fibres such as hessian, raffia and jute, while not strictly textiles, are another way to introduce touchy-feely texture to a scheme. Upholstered chairs and sofas will also up the cosy factor in a living space. Don't stop there though. Pile them high with cushions, blankets and throws in contrasting fabrics and layer, layer, layer for an instant mood of relaxation.

SOFT TO THE TOUCH

Adding textiles will soften the look and feel of a room as well as improving acoustics (*this page*). I like to include naturally dyed linen bedding and curtains in a bedroom, while patchwork is enjoying a resurgence in popularity and looks great used on cushions, bringing subtle detail to an interior, or to upholster a chair. Layer up beds and seating with woollen throws and sheepskins, and invest in lots of cushions – in my view, you can never have enough; they are the perfect way to add comfort, colour, pattern and, most of all, interest (*opposite and pages 30 and 31*).

CALMING
PATTERN

Pattern may not be the first ingredient that leaps to mind when putting together a tranquil interior, but the repetitive rhythms of smaller-scale patterns found in nature have been proven to reduce stress. There are many ways to use it in a calm interior – it's all about the type of pattern, how much you use and where you use it.

PATTERNED PERFECTION
The intricate plaiting/braiding of rush matting constitutes a pattern, but it's tonal and small scale, so more subtle than the geometric shapes of a cotton kilim, for example (*above left*). A faded vintage fabric will add muted interest without feeling jarring or overwhelming (*above centre*). Framed screen prints, or even pieces of fabric, will add a certain something to plain walls (*above right*), and in a living room scheme, just one patterned cushion or abstract rug may be all you need to add an extra decorative layer while retaining a room's inherent calming qualities (*opposite*).

MIX & MATCH

Mixing different patterns can be a challenge in a calm interior. The way to do it is to stick firmly to a very limited colour palette. The main pattern should be your 'hero', used on a sofa, a bedhead or a pair of curtains, then you can add a few pops of a less-complicated or small-scale print – a classic stripe or a ditsy floral or geometric design. Dilute these with lots of plains and textures so that the elements blend in rather than dominating. If you're using a neutral colour palette, you can mix more patterns because the tones are softer; a neutral geometric rug with patterned curtains and armchair, plain walls and sofa retains a simple, quiet look.

LAYERING UP

These schemes work because the patterns within the rooms add interest without being overpowering. A checked woollen blanket set among neutral tones and textures creates a focal point (*this page*), while classic stripes against a plain green linen sofa and neutral walls give colour and interest in a way that feels considered and clutter free (*opposite*).

CALMING
ELEMENTS

Look around you: your garden, a weekend walk or a day spent at the beach
will throw up all manner of natural elements that you can incorporate into
your decorative scheme. Such elements will add life and interest, and foster
a much-needed connection to nature that grounds and calms us.

NATURAL DETAILS

As an interiors stylist, I leap at any excuse to use fallen branches, found stones
and other natural objects in my work. Pretty much anything looks good: dried seed
heads, a single overblown rose, a gracefully shaped branch, bundles of foliage dead
or alive, pieces of driftwood, wild grasses, shells or pine cones. These natural objects
add just the right amount of interest, especially where an interior might be verging
on the minimal. Gather anything that takes your fancy in terms of colour or shape;
I guarantee it will add the essential finishing touch (*this page and opposite*).

NATURAL
OBJECTS

The beautiful natural forms of seashells, pebbles, dried hogweed or alliums, a feather or a gnarly, weathered lump of wood are all nature's works of art and, when displayed cleverly on a shelf, on a table, within a cabinet or as part of a group, can create soothing and harmonious sculptures that you'll never tire of. The texture, colour and patina of these treasures will add interest to any room. I like to display my natural treasures in groups of three or as single standout items. Mixing a variety of different objects in varying sizes can also work well for a textural still life. Sometimes keeping it simple is the key to a successful display, as it can be the textures and colour that make it appealing.

FINISHING FLOURISHES

Even the smallest of natural materials can do the trick. A simple sprig of honesty seed heads can be all that's needed (*opposite*), while the sculptural beauty of a fallen branch earns it pride of place on the wall in a hallway (*left*). In a city garden, a monumental old stone trough and deep borders surround a calm workspace where concentration will come easily (*above*). We are constantly reminded about the importance of nature to our mental health, so regardless of where you live, be sure to bring nature in (*above left*).

PLANTS & FLOWERS

In recent years, biophilia, or love of nature, has fuelled a huge trend for living with plants and flowers, and biophilic interior design focuses on bringing the sounds and textures of the natural world into the home. This has multiple benefits – living with plants not only looks good, but is also proven to reduce anxiety and even to boost our productivity. Biophilia can be as simple as buying flowers and nurturing pot plants, both of which can improve our health and well-being. House plants are an easy way to harness some of these gains, while even the smallest garden can offer up a few flowers. If you don't have a garden, swing by your local florist for a couple of stems to put on display. This look has nothing to do with showy arrangements of hothouse flowers, so keep it simple to powerful effect.

GOING GREEN

Plants and flowers will bring your home to life, whether your personal preference is for pot plants or cut flowers. Fill corners, shelves, even cupboards with pots and containers that are bursting with greenery, and fill favourite vases with a stem snipped from the garden or a local hedgerow (*this page and opposite*).

RESTORING ORDER

The way in which multiple possessions are organized will make all the difference between a calm and curated display and unruly and distracting clutter.

Regardless of what they are, if your belongings are arranged in a considered way, pretty much anything can look good – even household cleaning equipment. Items that fall into the same category always sit well together. You might have a collection of vintage ceramic jugs, for example, or it might be stoneware pots, glass vases or black and white photos.

Grouping items – pots, paintings, books – in threes is a fail-safe stylist's trick, but you can experiment with larger collections on dressers/hutches or open shelves to create a beautifully balanced installation. Opt for a restricted colour palette to maintain a calm vibe, but mix and match different sizes and add texture with vintage or handmade pieces. Stack kitchen- or glassware on shelves, or colour-match the spines of books. Less is more, as the saying goes, so if you're not sure, leave it out.

CURATED STYLE
We probably all desire a clutter-free home (I know I do!), so have a clear-out and sell excess stuff at a car boot/yard sale or give it to charity. Use your remaining favourite pieces to create vignettes that reflect your style. Assorted ceramics stacked on open shelves always look good, so don't feel you have to hide them away (*top left*). Artworks bring character and look charming whether hanging or propped against a wall (*top right, above right and opposite*), while a textile wall hanging takes centre stage when teamed with a few favourite items (*above left*).

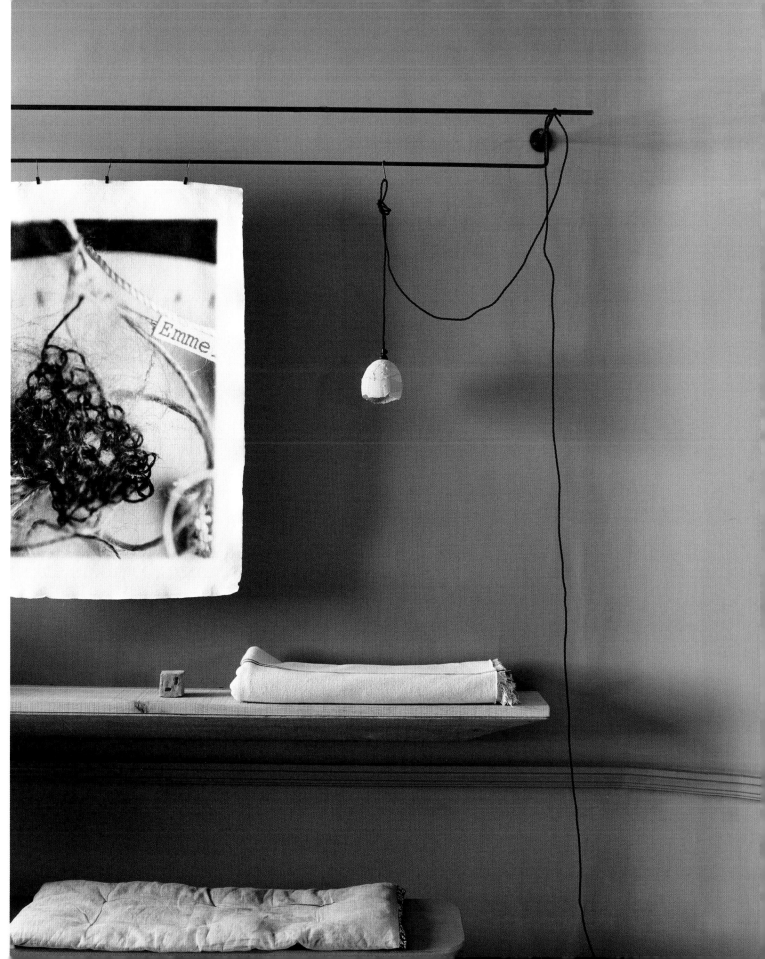

CALMING
INTERIORS

BEAUTIFULLY
CURATED

Josephine Ryan describes herself as an antiques dealer, interior designer, stylist and sometimes author; her style is honest and may look artfully thrown together, but is in fact thoughtfully and carefully curated.

The wonderful shop and home of Josephine Ryan Antiques in Tetbury, Gloucestershire has an interior that cocoons and envelops you the moment you step through the door from the busy high street. The beautiful Georgian facade, dating back to the 1760s, reeks of history and soul, but what is immediately noticeable upon entering are the paint colours used on the walls: soothing, tranquil and velvety tones that you want to reach out and touch them.

No. 44 Long Street is a Georgian extension to a Tudor house that still exists at the rear. From the front the dwelling looks huge; double fronted with three storeys, fourteen sash windows and an imposing colonnaded entrance, but the building is only one room deep, with generous proportions, original features and fireplaces.

'It is not really a residential building,' Josephine explains. 'It was being marketed as a shop or offices when I came upon it.

SERENE SHADES
The main living room-cum-showroom space is on the first floor and painted Drab Green by Edward Bulmer Natural Paint (*above and opposite*). This muted hue creates a room with depth and sophistication, perfect as a backdrop for antiques. Painting walls and woodwork/trim the same tone creates a sense of serenity, as the eyes travel across the space without interruption.

HOME FROM HOME
Artworks, plants, fresh flowers, foliage and dried flowers are dotted among the antiques for sale (*pages 48 and 49*). A primitive wooden table and Belgian oil painting set against natural painted walls and flagstone floors creates a retail experience that feels more like visiting a friend than walking round a shop (*left*).

GOING UP
The wooden staircase leads up to the private rooms on the top floor (*opposite*). The upper rooms all have their original floorboards, which provide a timeless setting for an array of antique furniture, rugs, artworks and vintage lamps.

The only way I could consider running my business from there, given my main home and family are in London, was if I could stay while at work.' The space doesn't have a 'proper' kitchen and only a shower, but 'I absolutely love being there,' Josephine tells me. 'At night when the shop is closed, it is magical. I sit in the smallest room, painted in a serene shade called Drab Green, with the fire and candles lit and the shutters firmly closed, and I feel like I'm in a period drama!' she laughs. There are four rooms on two floors, a large hallway with stone slab flooring and a magnificent sweeping staircase leading to a generous upstairs landing/hallway. All the rooms are used as showroom space, displaying furniture, mirrors and art in room settings. The top floor has three rooms, one for storage and the other two private.

When Josephine moved in she didn't need to decorate, as naturally pigmented heritage paints by Edward Bulmer already covered the walls, offering the perfect muted backdrop for her ever-changing stock. However, she points out, 'When one of the rooms needed redecorating recently, I repainted it in a versatile Fawn colour, also by Edward Bulmer, that is much more in keeping with my palette.'

Tetbury, well known for its many fine antiques dealers and design shops, is a place where Josephine feels right at home. 'This property has given me the opportunity to trial not being in the city, and I actually love it,' she declares, adding that if she could, she would install an old rolltop tub on the top floor, tank the cellar and install a Plain English kitchen complete with a large white AGA.

Josephine's love of items with a time-worn patina helps to bring a calm mood to the interior, and she confesses to always falling for 'the frayed edges of used silk curtains or foxing in mirrors'. The house is full of natural materials: linen bedding, painted floorboards and scrubbed wooden tables. Old mirrors you can't see yourself in and battered pewter are key to her style, along with fresh flowers or foraged foliage, 'a single bloom or a lichen-covered branch' that brings life to a scheme and connects with nature. 'You can never have too many vases, displayed thoughtfully on a shelf – when not in use they can look interesting,' she explains.

When it comes to decorating, Josephine's advice is to 'work with the period architecture of the room you are decorating. Every environment requires a different treatment, but most importantly develop your own personal style.' Paint bare wood furniture, limewash walls, build bespoke cupboards with salvaged antique fronts and install unpolished (but sealed) stone or granite worktops that show their inherent beauty and natural pigments. Use natural fibres, in particular linen, which has an earthiness and sophistication that works beautifully as curtains, gives texture to upholstery and as bedlinen is luxurious. But most importantly, 'Take inspiration from everywhere – on a bus, a country walk, art galleries – and remember what delights you. Don't discount junk shops and boot fairs/yard sales, and don't be afraid to ring the bell of an antiques shop either!'

CLASSIC COMBINATION
The dining space has a fresher scheme, with sky-blue walls and off-white shutters and woodwork/trim creating an airy, open mood (*opposite and above*). Antique dining furniture takes centre stage here, while the large fireplace is flanked by two large linen-upholstered armchairs, one of which used to be a favourite spot for Josephine's beloved dog Ted. Light pours in through the tall sash windows and two beautiful old mirrors bounce it around the room.

THE ART OF DISPLAY

When it comes to display, less is definitely more in a calm interior. Team similar pieces, shapes or colours together on shelves, a mantelpiece or tabletop. Glass vases, bowls and decanters work well with and without flowers, and a shelving unit can be a good way of corralling lots of items without looking bitty or busy (*opposite*). Or play with scale to create a striking focal point, as with this single oversized piece of dried foliage popped in a huge urn (*this page*).

TRANQUIL PINK

In the main bedroom, walls have been painted in Jonquil by Edward Bulmer Natural Paint (*this page and opposite*). A restful yellow-pink reminiscent of gypsum plaster, it is not sugary but muted in tone. These eco-friendly paints allow old walls and woodwork to breathe and offer a slightly textured effect rather than flat, solid colour.

TRANQUIL
VIEWS

This little house perched on the side of a hill in the village of Coverack on the south-east coast of Cornwall is the perfect space in which to pause and take stock. Not only does it look straight out to sea, but the elements inside are considered, simple and comfortable, making a restful home that's ideal for contemplation and relaxation. The owner Simon Francis and his family rebuilt the house with this ethos in mind.

With help from Kathryn Tyler of Linea Studio, who designed and managed the project, and Gekko Designs property renovation specialists, the project was complete within two years. Simon and family bought the property in August 2018 and renovations were finished in July 2020. He describes his style as modern with a homely, laid-back feel and says, 'All the guests who have stayed have said how calm it is – an oasis in a lovely little fishing village.' He continues, 'To me it's all about the sea view, with the headland adding contrast. When the prevailing wind is from the west, the sea beyond the headland behaves differently to the sea that's

OUTSIDE IN
The open-plan living space with huge picture windows framed with low-level seating draws your eyes straight out to sea rather than blocking it with bulky pieces of furniture (*opposite*). The neutral tones of the interior woods, linens, sisals, grey floor tiles and Clayworks plaster walls are echoed in the muted colours of the sea, rocks, foliage and coastal path, creating a seamless visual blend between the two (*this page*).

OPEN-PLAN LIVING
The interior is simple with a wood burner for winter nights, simple furniture in neutral tones and lots of low-level sisal, wooden and woven furniture (*opposite*). The fuss-free scheme creates a mood of peace and serenity, and works in tandem with the rugged coastal path, rocks and fauna outside. Here again the walls were treated in Clayworks plaster, which has a textured appearance (*this page*).

KITCHEN ORDERLY

The kitchen is homely but has a modern twist with floating open shelving that houses everyday tableware (*right*). It sits at the back of the open-plan ground floor to make the most of the outstanding view out to sea (*opposite*). The dining area is in the middle, connecting the kitchen and living areas with tonal colours, dark chairs and complementary accessories so that the whole space works as a whole (*below*). Everything here is simple, uncluttered and fuss free.

protected by it, and added to that the diving gannets, seals and dolphins that we regularly see ensure that it's a captivating view.'

The interior is modern but far from clinical; it's warm and layered with a contemporary twist. Simon comments, 'A lot of the furniture is second hand or reclaimed, which helps to create a warmer feel within the space. I'm a big fan of our coffee table in the sitting room, which is an old praying bed from Africa's Ivory Coast.'

The house was built in the 1960s and was lived in by the same family for nearly 40 years. Simon wanted to retain the boxy exterior, but the internal layout was completely reconfigured, with new windows and a larger side door onto the garden. Architecturally, the family were keen to redefine the building's exterior and wanted an exterior wooden cladding that would silver and mellow into the vernacular of the village, so they chose a sustainably sourced Siberian larch cladding with subtle fins that catch the light and cast ever-changing shadows throughout the day.

A SEA VIEW

The master suite is a sight to behold with a mix of warm toning woods, leather chairs, textured linens, a freestanding wood-clad bathtub and statement lighting, but the true hero piece is the picture window beyond the tub that looks out to sea (*right*). Nothing here detracts from the view; instead, the harmonious natural tones, materials and shapes draw your eye to the seascape beyond. A reclining chair allows you to take stock and admire the view (*opposite*).

The house was completely rewired, an air source heat pump was installed, windowsills were dropped almost to floor level to increase the size of the window openings, and weather-proof aluminium window frames were fitted. Downstairs, new floor tiles were laid with underfloor heating and a new kitchen by David Restorick was installed, as well as a wood burner. The walls and ceilings were finished in Clayworks clay plaster to give a pared-back yet tactile feel, with curved edges to soften the effect.

Simon describes the interior as influenced by Scandinavian summer houses and the Japanese sensibilities of architect George Nakashima, and it draws upon a simple palette of concrete, linen and timber. 'We designed and decorated in close collaboration with Kathryn Tyler and were on the same page regarding the look we were trying to achieve. I gave her free rein and said yes to all her design suggestions, as she understood what we were trying to achieve,' Simon explains.

The downstairs living area is a large open-plan space with a kitchen at one end, a dining table in the middle and the main seating area at the other end with stunning views out over the water. French doors open directly onto

a paved and gravelled terrace softened with abundant plants and flowers, and the natural stone colours here merge seamlessly with the house's wood-clad exterior.

Upstairs, the bedrooms are simple but cleverly planned, with interesting detailing such as hessian fabric on the wooden doors, built-in shelving to create a sense of order and lots of clean-lined furniture and storage that keeps the rooms light and uncluttered. This upper floor was reconfigured to accommodate two new en-suite bathrooms and a wonderful freestanding bathtub was installed in front of the huge picture window in the master bedroom, which Simon says is one of his favourite spots. The repeated use of natural materials and neutral shades brings a tranquil vibe to this blissful retreat. Restful and serene, it is a home to be proud of.

DESIGN HEROES

The bedrooms and bathrooms are designed to make the most of the limited space and the best of the stunning views (*this page and opposite*). Instead of bulky closets, there is open storage for clothes, with peg rails and shelving to keep the rooms clutter-free (*opposite above right and below*). Furniture is kept to a minimum, and the subtle natural colours blend harmoniously to create a seamless sense of unity throughout.

COASTAL DREAMING

Sally and Edward's Devon home is the coastal house of dreams and has won a whole host of architectural awards to prove it. Having spent many years walking past the house with their young family, the couple had always admired its position and the property had even come up for sale, but not at the right time. More recently, however, the house came on the market again, and this time they jumped at the chance to own it.

'Dan Pearson created a wonderful master plan for the whole estate and a detailed landscape design for the garden,' Edward explains. 'His vision was to connect the house to the landscape and the sea via the garden. It was Dan who introduced us to Stephanie Macdonald at 6a architects. Steph saw the opportunity to reconnect the old house to the landscape using its stone walls.'

ROOM TO BREATHE
The stone walls are painted with Farrow & Ball's Slipper Satin distemper, which has a flat, powdery appearance (*this page and opposite*). Soaring windows, a high ceiling and multiple natural textures create a space that is serene and restful. The glass coffee table hosts coastal collections, while artworks add gentle colour to a neutral canvas.

The house occupies a remarkable position, with extensive views of the sea and the South Devon coast. Previously it was an unremarkable early-20th century structure, but it has been transformed: stripped back to its thick stone walls, insulated externally and then clad in reclaimed Delabole slate. Positioned on a coastal path in an Area of Outstanding Natural Beauty, a consideration in the design brief was to retain the character of the exterior of the house. 'It was important to us to keep the exterior the same,' Sally observes. 'The house is quite prominent and we didn't want to ruin people's memories of it, or disturb the shape too much.' The only major external changes were subtle additions afforded by the cladding, including a cast-lead fascia to the eaves and recessed external window seats outside the kitchen.

Inside, the stone walls were revealed for the first time, but they have been softened by the application of a lime slurry to preven crumbling. Steph completely reconfigured the interior, with new timber stairs and balconies that wind around the old chimney cores to create double-height rooms and triple-height top-lit hallways. The effect is breathtaking while remaining cosy and calm. The rooms are filled with artworks,

SOARING SPACES

The double-height living room is framed by a huge oak column (*opposite*). The mezzanine level overlooking this area doubles as Sally's study, while a sunken space at the back of the room houses the piano and library. Painted stone walls are combined with wooden tongue-and-groove panelling (*above right*). 6a architects responded to Sally's love of trees in the views from every window. In the dining room, an original window was enlarged to frame a wonderful oak tree (*right*).

ROOM WITH A VIEW
The sleek, clean lines of the kitchen are set off by chunky oak beams and a primitive comb-back armchair from Robert Young Antiques (*above left and right*). A sisal rug and mid-century dining chairs make comfortable additions to this space (*opposite*). Scout the dog looks out towards the garden, landscaped by Dan Pearson. The flowers on the table are from Sally's cutting garden.

primitive West Country armchairs and other interesting decorative elements. 'I took some inspiration from Kettle's Yard, and its simplicity,' admits Sally.

Originally the house was raised on a plinth, but this was lowered to ground level and a chimney breast removed, absorbing the old hallway into the living room and increasing its size, resulting in a part-barn, part-country house feel, with tall, elongated openings where the old windows once were. The masonry reveals clues to the room's previous form, as fireplaces have become wall recesses and joist supports are now low-level shelving.

With three floors at the north end of the house connecting to two floors at the south, each space has a distinct volume and ceiling height, with the central staircase giving three views through the house: from the front door through the dining room to the oak tree in the garden; from the back door through the hall and living room to the sea; and from the centre of the hall vertically up to the sky. 'Every room connects to the landscape. We use the covered verandah every day, whether for breakfast at the weekends or for a drink in the evening, whatever the weather,' explains Edward.

QUIET INTERIORS
Sally's desk sits on the open mezzanine above the large living space and looks out to the sea (*opposite*). The architects' models and artwork dotted around add interest (*left*). The house pays respect to the landscape through its use of local and natural materials and its pared-back decor (*below*). There are no curtains to block the view on the seaward side, only white shutters.

Air-dried oak beams create an exposed structure between the existing stone walls, while larger structural elements were made from cast in-situ concrete. Sustainably sourced tapered oak verticals are a recurrent theme throughout, from the large column in the drawing room to the verandah posts and even the staircase spindles.

The architects' decision to retain the original thick stone walls brought significant environmental benefits. They stabilize the temperature inside the house, keeping it warm in winter and cool on the hottest summer days. The building is wrapped with wood-fibre insulation beneath locally sourced reclaimed slates, maintaining the breathability of the construction. 'Attaching 200mm/8in of insulation to the outside of the building then reapplying the vertical tiles has achieved 21st-century thermal properties in a house that still reveals its 19th-century origins,' Edward says. The couple agree that the house is a haven, providing a calm, contemplative connection with the garden and the sea beyond.

CALMING ZONES

The decoration has been kept deliberately simple in the
bedroom and bathroom, where a freestanding bathtub takes
centre stage. The bathroom is one of the few rooms with a
muted pastel shade on the wall, and the tall window overlooks
trees and the surrounding landscape (*above and above right*).
Primitive chairs, artworks and linen bedding, along with
architectural details such as the exposed timber grounds in
the plasterwork, create a relaxed bedroom (*right and opposite*).

GEORGIAN GEM

This beautiful Georgian terraced building, built around 1810, stands in the heart of Marylebone in central London. Its lofty ceilings and generous windows make the interior extremely light and bright, a feature that owners Elise and Stephen never fail to appreciate. The couple have lived in the area since they married in 1996, starting out in a one-bedroom flat just around the corner: 'We loved that flat, but had to leave when the children arrived.' In November 2002 they moved into this house and have been there ever since.

When the couple bought the building it was an accountant's office, with flouncy curtains hanging at the windows and wall-to-wall carpets with floral borders. Stephen, an architect who set up Works Architecture in 2000, designed and carried out a full refurbishment before they moved in. 'The parts of the house that we have occupied have changed a lot through the years,' recalls Elise, who is also an architect. 'Initially, we divided the building into four apartments and lived on the ground and first floors. As our family grew, we took over the basement and lived on three floors.

DARK AND HANDSOME

The ground floor is the darkest part of the house. Elise and Stephen have played on this by painting both rooms in Farrow & Ball's Oval Room Blue, a rich greeny-blue. There are spots of deep red in the furnishings for a pop of unexpected colour, and the reduced light and deep tones make this a wonderfully cosy space to snuggle up in or enjoy drinks with friends (*this page and opposite*).

HIGH WINDOWS

This elegant living space on the first floor is where the family spend the majority of their time. Large windows fill the room with light, while low-level seating encourages a relaxed vibe. Elise's love of craft is evident here, with handcrafted foliage wreaths and natty mobiles along with a family album of Polaroid snaps that has evolved into an artwork in its own right (*this page and opposite*).

Finally, eight years ago, we reconfigured everything and now live in the whole house, with a flat that we rent out in the basement.'

The couple wanted to keep the interior as pared back and simple as possible. 'As with most of our projects, we were after simplicity,' Elise remarks. 'These houses are so glorious in themselves that we feel that it is best to make the most of the original features and apply the lightest of touches so as not to mask any of the original glory.' The large living room on the first floor is also the kitchen and dining area, and is where the family tend to spend most time together. This is the lightest, brightest area of the house, with soaring ceilings and beautiful original cornicing/moldings. 'We stripped away 200 years of paint from the cornice to reveal the very ornate and intricate design,' Elise remembers.

The house was originally divided up into many smaller rooms, so the biggest change was to open up spaces to give the family more flexibility in how they use the house, as well as the ability to rearrange the furniture from time

NATURE LOVER

Wherever you look, Elise has brought nature inside. Flowers adorn the dining table and foliage finds are popped into vases or made into delicate still lifes (*this page and opposite*). This link between indoors and out is important, as being close to nature is proven to reduce stress. Soft off-white walls, delicate blue linens and simple furniture finish off this restful and calming space.

green, grey-pink. We have balanced light walls with dark woodwork [trim] and warmer shades of grey elsewhere. The white is a soft white/light grey and the black is a soft black/very dark grey, with varying tones and intensities in between.'

Elise's sense of style is evident in every room: little ceramic signs, beautiful handmade lights and foraged foliage are dotted around. 'I have made a lot of the furnishings and fittings around the house; other treasured pieces were made by family or close friends. These are the things that make it feel like our home and no-one else's. I like making 'clusters' – lights or candles, a shelf or a table, sometimes a mirror and perhaps a stool or a bench. There is always an opportunity to make a nice display and then that becomes my favourite spot in the house, until the next one comes along,' she smiles.

All the rooms in the house exude a strong sense of calm. The lower floors feature more colour and decorative detail, while the main bedroom and dressing area on the top floor are the quietest in feel. 'There is little going on in terms of decor; they are very simple, quiet spaces,' Elise remarks. She feels that a sense of continuity is key to the success of the scheme. 'We have the same timber floor running throughout the house, including the kitchen and bathrooms. The walls are the same colour throughout and we have either simple white metro tiles or painted brickwork in the wet areas.'

The secret to this mood of soothing serenity? Elise would suggest picking one favourite object and building your room around it, whether it be a lamp, a sofa, a painting – even a scrap of fabric. Choose something that makes you feel happy, calm and relaxed, and you won't go far wrong.

to time. 'The building is Grade II listed, so we had to work within certain restrictions,' says Elise. 'But this didn't stop previous owners throwing the original fireplaces into a skip/dumpster!'

Colour choices were carefully considered. 'Shades of grey make me feel calm and happy and the palette is limited, which means it's easy to mix and match items and move things around. Within all of this, an element of rich, deep colour or pattern stops things becoming too dull,' explains Elise. 'I love blues and greens, but mostly I love grey. Pretty much everything we have sits within a broad grey spectrum: grey-blue, grey-

STILL LIFE

Little vignettes, which Elise calls her 'clusters', appear throughout the house (*this page*). They are testament to Elise's love of curation and her sense of order, which is so important for a house that feels serene. Everything in its place is the order of the day. Even the bikes are neatly tucked away out of sight under the stairs (*opposite*).

ROOM AT THE TOP

The top floor is where Elise and Stephen work and sleep, and according to Elise it's the 'calmest part of the house'. The limited colour palette and sloping roof in the bedroom make it supremely restful, while a closet on the landing/upstairs hallway keeps the space uncluttered (*left and opposite*). Elise says, 'I think my top tip would be to play around with lighting. This makes and changes spaces so easily, and is a super-simple way to create mood and atmosphere.' (*above and above left*)

CONTEMPORARY COTTAGE

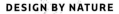

DESIGN BY NATURE
A strip of inset cobble flooring runs along the French windows in the kitchen, adding interest and texture and echoing the cobbles outside (*above and opposite*). Annabelle designed the oak-framed roof overhang to create an outside seating area as well as storage for logs, blankets and wellies. The wood-clad walls, painted brick, wooden furniture and abundance of plants and foliage all combine to create a natural, textural space that links inside and out (*above right*).

Walking through the door of Annabelle and David's home in Cheshire, you are immediately struck by the textures and character of the building's fabric: the worn beams, distressed brickwork, sleek ply, pebble floors and painted woodwork all exude tranquillity, warmth and patina.

An architect by trade who launched her own practice, Annabelle Tugby Architects, in 2011, Annabelle has transformed a Tudor cottage in need of renovation into a cosy contemporary home for herself and her partner, her three children, three cats and Otto the dog. The cottage forms part of an estate surrounding a hall and bordered by farmland. 'Our house was the dower house and has beautiful views over a mini Stonehenge and various other follies.' When Annabelle came to view the property, she had no idea about the garden or views because it was so overgrown. She had already lived elsewhere in the village, but had never known about this part, so it was a pleasant surprise. Built in the 1700s, 'The house offered all the comforts of my old home, but with an opportunity to renovate the whole house to my own brief.'

The previous owners shared their happy memories of the house, which made Annabelle fall in love with them and the house at the same time. Maggie and Marshall,

A WARM WELCOME

Inspired by a hotel she visited in the Alps, Annabelle hung a luxuriously heavy curtain in the entrance hall to screen the front door. The original beams add to the sense of character. She covered the floor with natural fibre matting (*opposite*). 'I particularly love the seagrass flooring, as it is so forgiving to the shape of our old floors,' Annabelle says. Describing the living room, she continues, 'I brought the cotton-covered sofas from Sofa.com from my last home and the bronze round table (*right*). The seagrass ties everything together with lamps and a selection of books, plants and family photographs.'

the previous owners, agreed to a sale, and after completion in August 2018, the renovations began. The house had to be underpinned to allow for the insertion of a large contemporary kitchen with enough height to retain the beautiful original oak floor joists that they uncovered above. Part of the old cruck frame (the curved timber that supports the roof of the building) was discovered, and this was carefully cleaned and left exposed in its original location in the kitchen.

The house is made of painted brick on the low sections with timber framing up to the eaves, and has a pitched roof of rosemary clay tiles. Architecturally, the main

challenge was creating a design to replace the leaking flat-roofed extension next to the kitchen with something that complemented the cottage and provided practical additional space. Annabelle designed an oak frame to the same width, with an overhang to the front that houses a table, a doorway and a boot room area and, at the back, a glasshouse where the old conservatory used to be. Other renovations included digging out the floors of the kitchen and utility room, putting on a new roof, rewiring and replumbing, reglazing all the windows with heritage glass and redecorating all the brickwork and the repairs to the oak framing.

SMOOTH TO THE TOUCH

The unexpected use of plywood in this Tudor cottage is a clever contemporary touch. All along one side of the kitchen, ply conceals built-in cupboards and lines shelves that hold glasses, cups and other kitchenware (*above and opposite*). The smooth surface and calm tone of the light processed wood add another layer of texture and interest to the kitchen while blending seamlessly into the design.

Annabelle even designed the steel and glass patio doors and the internal cobble floors, 'which I laid around the house, to replace the concrete paviours'. Her designs have brought texture to every room, with a cohesive colour palette: '80% cream, 15% timber, 5% black', she explains. When it came to decorating, Annabelle chose Farrow & Ball's Wimborne White for both inside and out, using it externally on the plasterwork and painted brick as well as throughout the interior, across all the walls, woodwork/trim and even as a wash on the exposed brickwork.

The lighting was a major part of the design process. The kitchen, for example, was fitted with several different levels of lighting to create the desired atmosphere at different moments during the day. 'I have lighting in the cupboards, which are wonderful at night after dinner, under the shelves and the booth seats, at the back of the worktop and up the exposed brick wall to enhance the texture, and in the corners of the room to increase the size of the space. The only visible light fitting is the track light with movable spotlights, which are useful when preparing meals,' Annabelle explains.

She admits that it's been an enormous pleasure creating something new and embracing natural materials in her designs. 'I want to look at a piece of furniture or a part of the house and for it to have a sense of history. Materials such as wood, stone, brick, wool, lime and timber are all essential to me,' she explains. 'These are the architectural backbone of the design, and when a room is empty, it should still exude character while being a calming and healthy environment in which to live. When this is right, adding extra decorative elements is always successful.'

A CALMING KITCHEN

The dual-aspect kitchen with its exposed brick wall has separate zones for dining, sitting and cooking (*this page and opposite*). There is a practical kitchen island in the centre and a large opening to the dining space, which is home to an old limed mahogany table left by the previous owners (*see page 93*). Annabelle says her favourite spot in the house is the breakfast space in the kitchen (*below*). 'I occasionally get to enjoy a cup of tea in the window enjoying the view, but usually we squeeze in for intimate meals,' she smiles. Comfortable, sociable and welcoming, the cosy ply-lined booth is a replica of one Annabelle saw in a Manchester restaurant and has become the heart of the kitchen.

THE TRANQUIL ZONE
The master bedroom is decorated in shades of white
to enhance the sense of light and space. A fine antique
bed is the main focal point and grounds the off-white walls,
linen bedding and woollen throw (*this page*). In the en-suite
bathroom, the old bathtub, which had wonderful views
over the fields, was replaced with a freestanding tub in the
same position. A large antique mirror bounces light around
the room and adds decorative interest (*opposite*).

RURAL HIDEAWAY

TRADITIONAL TEXTURES

A mix of slate, stone and carefully chosen paint colours combine to create a house that sits quietly within its surroundings. The original stone walls were restored and break up the tongue-and-groove panelling to create focal points throughout the ground-floor rooms (*above*). Furniture is simple and considered, and the colours and materials have been chosen to create a timeless interior where nothing distracts or overpowers (*opposite and above right*). It is a tranquil environment in which to sit, relax and dream.

Nicola, the owner of this house, says that her style has been described as 'straddling the line between past and present'. Stepping inside her stunning Welsh farmhouse in a quiet valley at the edge of the Cambrian Mountains, I immediately understand why. Nicola has cleverly combined modern functional design with muted natural colours, rugged exposed stonework, reclaimed materials and repurposed elements that look and feel entirely sympathetic to their surroundings, and create a nurturing environment for the owners to enjoy.

The remote, off-grid home is a cosy retreat for the most wonderful family consisting of Nicola, an artist, her professor husband, three children, five hens, two ducks, two cats and a dog. They bought the Victorian-era, traditional Welsh farmhouse with cart house and barn a number of years ago now. 'The house was derelict when we purchased it, and had been empty for over 25 years,' Nicola explains. 'The roof had caved in and the walls were collapsing, so the first job was to remove all the dangerous bits, which meant we were literally left with four stone walls and window voids!'

The main challenges were the difficult access to the property and the fact it was off-grid. Trying to persuade

NEXT TO NATURE

Nicola painted the panelled walls in colours that mirror the natural elements outside. In the living room, a deep forest green creates a cocooning backdrop for the slate floor and slouchy sofa. Large artworks add impact but don't overwhelm (*this page*). The open door offers a pleasing glimpse of a lighter tonal green in the hallway and kitchen (*opposite and pages 102 and 103*).

contractors to travel down a long, rocky track and across a ford was a huge task in itself, so the couple ended up carrying out a lot of the work themselves, with the help of friends and trusted local builders. 'It took quite a few years before we set up a hydro scheme that would give us electricity on site. Prior to that we used a generator for power tools and a solar panel for computers and phones, with candles for lighting,' Nicola remembers.

To help insulate the exposed building, a new frame was constructed within the stone walls, leaving a cavity between the existing stone and the new internal cladding.

Nicola bought a nail gun and painstakingly installed wooden tongue-and-groove panelling to most of the walls and ceilings. 'It gives a great acoustic and warmth,' she explains. The remainder of the existing stone walls was left exposed, which helps to connect the house to the outdoors. 'What attracted us to the house was its relationship to the surrounding environment,' Nicola reflects. 'The previous tenants, who were born here, have visited us and shared stories of sheep shearing, baking days and the doctor visiting on horseback.' This is a home that has been well loved over the centuries.

Nicola wanted the house to feel restful, warm and welcoming. She chose a muted colour palette that is reminiscent of the surrounding landscape and painted the panelling in natural pigments. 'Being up in the hills with lots of mud around, white was not an option and I wanted the colours to relate from one room to the next.' She used linseed oil paint, mainly from Brouns & Co and Swedish Linseed Paint, mixing the colours herself. 'I've even named some of the colours after close friends,' Nicola smiles.

Her love of rustic surfaces such as unlacquered brass, slate and wood is evident in the house. 'I love using natural materials that improve with age. We used slate for the floor downstairs and oak boards upstairs in the bedrooms and bathroom. The panelling against the stone walls is a lovely contrast. The house has always had a great atmosphere with its tactile surfaces, and now it's warm, with underfloor heating powered by the hydro and wood burners in the living room and kitchen,' Nicola says. When it came to lighting, they installed lots of low-level light and a system that can build by turning on more lights when needed. 'After a long time using candles, we decided to keep the electric wattage low when it was eventually introduced to maintain a cosy atmosphere.'

Nicola's design ethos is key to the success of this beautiful interior. She says that she believes in 'nurturing the things you love and working with them. You often have what you need already. Sometimes taking things away is a better option than buying more.' I couldn't agree more.

KITCHEN COMFORT

The sage green kitchen has a long refectory table surrounded by mismatched chairs, a wood-burning stove and open shelving for crockery, glassware and kitchenware (*pages 102 and 103*). 'I had the kitchen sink made to a traditional style, and the rest of the kitchen we made from things we found on site or had left over,' Nicola says.

RESTFUL NIGHTS

All the bedrooms are clutter free, with under-bed storage and painted in a palette of soothing shades for a restful mood (*opposite, above and page 107*). Traditional Welsh blankets cover the beds.

SOOTHING SPACE
In the bathrooms, Nicola fitted reclaimed sanitary ware, including this freestanding claw-foot tub (*page 106*).

A TRANQUIL WELCOME
Max the dog surveys the scene from the large hallway, which has slate floors and ample hanging space for hats, coats, boots and pet paraphernalia. Nicola painted the panelled walls with natural pigments and linseed paint from Brouns & Co and Swedish Linseed Paint to mirror the colours of the natural elements outside (*left and opposite*).

A CLEAN
SLATE

After moving to London from Seoul in 2012, Johan and Frida had been house-hunting for just under a year when they discovered this calm, quiet street set in a busy South London suburb. 'We liked the area because the houses and gardens are spacious and the location is quite central with good transport links. It was also important to have enough space for Frida's studio, as she works and teaches from home,' Johan explains. The couple's house is part of a modern development that was completed in 2006, but its classical architectural style is in line with houses in the surrounding streets that were built in the 1840s.

Having purchased the property in July 2018, the refurbishment began in March 2019. Frida and Johan bought the house with the clear intention to extend the kitchen. 'This was always a risk,' explains Johan, 'as planning permission was required. However, we mitigated this by hiring a planning consultant early on for both the kitchen and the garden studio.'

The project wasn't a case of a quick facelift or simple refresh. Rather, the couple planned major changes. Perhaps the biggest

CREATIVE SPACE
A gnarly old walnut tree at the bottom of the garden frames a wooden garden studio designed by Ecospace Studios (*above*). Floral designer Frida's 'indoors' studio is on the ground floor of the house and has a cool stone floor and no heating. The subdued tone and velvety texture of the plastered walls makes them the ideal backdrop for her stunning floral sculptures (*opposite*).

KEEP CALM
In the living room, the carpet is from Bazaar
Velvet and the sofa from Loaf, while the Italian
travertine coffee table came from Maison
Artefact. Linen curtains by Govindia Hemphill
frame the window (*this page and opposite
right*). The antique mantelpiece was found
by Victoria Davar of Maison Artefact (*opposite
left*). Frida's floral arrangements take pride
of place, a piece of art in their own right.

was the large kitchen extension, which now projects out into the garden. The rest of the house was stripped back to the walls, ceilings and floors, and changes were also made to the layout and windows. The staircase was rebuilt, windows were enlarged and one was added in the entrance hall. In addition, a stairwell to the front lightwell was added, the lower-ground utility room was rearranged and many other tweaks were made so that the house would work perfectly for its new owners. A garden studio requiring separate planning permission was constructed and, last but not least, the garden underwent a complete redevelopment by garden designer Jane Brockbank and Will Wright Landscapes, which also required approval, as the house sits in a conservation area.

Key design decisions were made early on. Dinesen classic oak boards finished with white oil run throughout most of the house, and all the walls were finished with Clayworks plaster rather than paint. The lighting was carefully planned and designed with the help of lighting designer Richard Aldridge at Roundlight. Johan and Frida wanted the technology to be 'hidden and seamless', so there are speakers concealed in the kitchen ceiling as well as the living room and master bathroom, and the lights and underfloor heating are controlled via an app.

The result is a soulful, simple and seamless home that the couple describe as something of a team effort. 'We knew antiques dealer and designer Victoria Davar from Maison Artefact very well and she introduced us to our architect Richard Eden of Edenkido, who was involved in all technical aspects along with the interior design, even down to the light-switches. The four of us formed the core team and were involved in all matters throughout

QUIET DINING

The Tobi-Ishi dining table in grey cement is by Edward Barber & Jay Osgerby for B&B Italia with dining chairs by Fritz Hansen from Conran. The corner cabinet was sourced by Victoria Davar and is one of Frida and Johan's favourite pieces. The Rio In and Out suspension light is by Kaia Lighting and the large artwork by British painter Deborah Tarr. The elements were carefully chosen to blend seamlessly and create a beautifully serene area in which to eat.

SHADES OF GREY

The soft off-whites and greys of the kitchen combine to create a delightfully tranquil area. The Vincent Van Duysen kitchen was chosen from Molteni&C/Dada with a natural stone countertop from Italy (*above*). Frida and daughter Myung love the steps outside the kitchen – the best place from which to observe the garden beyond. Richard the architect explains, 'The garden steps create a wonderful picture window to focus your view across the island out to the garden, the picture always changing.' (*opposite*).

the project,' Johan says. After the purchase of the property was finalized, Johan started a scrapbook of images of designs, colours and textures that he liked, which became the reference point for the overall design. Inspiration was drawn from Belgian designers Vincent Van Duysen and Axel Vervoordt, known for their restful, pared-back interiors, and Johan reveals that a quote by Vincent Van Duysen captured the vision for this home: 'Architectural creation should be a place where the spiritual and material world are one'.

With all these thoughts in place, a clear 'design language' developed, based on a restricted palette of colours, materials and textures that flow almost seamlessly from space to space. Designing the house as if it was one big room rather than lots of different ones is the secret behind the calm, timeless mood of the interior. Texture is key to the sense of tranquillity: the plaster walls, oiled wooden floors, antique pieces and the use of metal and brass, along with Frida's flowers, make this a very special environment to live in. The couple decided not to bring their old furniture to their new home, instead wanting a fresh slate, but the desire to combine old and new was important and Victoria Davar from Maison Artefact was key to sourcing exactly the right pieces for each room.

Johan sums up how the house makes the couple feel: 'At peace, relaxing, almost monastic; there is a calming energy throughout the house. We were fortunate that we could start with an almost completely blank canvas and create our own space, including the most amazing garden. We absolutely love it, almost to the point of having no reason to leave – it feels like a real sanctuary,' he smiles.

REST EASY

In the tranquil master bedroom, a bed by Molteni & C/ Dada takes centre stage, dressed with soothing earth-toned linens from Larusi (*this page*). In the bathroom, a water-repellent tadelakt finish is combined with Dinesen classic oak cladding around the bathtub and on the floor. It's the ultimate place to relax (*opposite*).

SOOTHING SEASIDE

My family's seaside bolthole on the East Coast of England is where we go to press the reset button. I've drawn on my skills as a stylist to create a welcoming, laid-back home that gives us a sense of calm the moment we walk through the door.

The original two-up, two-down cottage, which is part of a red-brick terrace built in 1904, sits in the heart of the seaside town of Southwold on the Suffolk coast. We love the simplicity of the coast here, and it's a place that helps to recharge and revive us every time we visit. The beach is just a few minutes' walk away, which is one of the reasons we love it so much – we don't need to drive anywhere.

For many years we lived with the decor of the previous owners, complete with polystyrene tiles, Formica shelving units, net curtains and blown vinyl floral wallpaper in the kitchen. When we began to think about renovating and creating a bigger living space, we knew we would first have to tackle the layout. The original cottage had a living room at the front with a small kitchen and bathroom at the rear. Upstairs there were three bedrooms, each leading into another.

VARIED TEXTURES
Classic ticking on the armchair and a pop of yellow linen add interest to the pared-back all-white scheme in the living space, where the walls and woodwork are painted in Linen Wash by Little Greene (*left and above left*). The garden cabin is made with an oak frame and clad in recycled boards with a corrugated roof. The table was made from the old kitchen roof joists (*opposite*).

DINING ZONE
In the kitchen, I designed a banquette (painted in Little Greene's Lamp Black eggshell) for the dining space that overlooks the back garden, softening it with a ticking-stripe seat pad and lots of linen cushions (*this page*). Light fittings from Tinsmiths plus vintage pictures and ceramics from Dantes Ceramics and Ben Baglio add an earthy warmth to the table (*opposite*). Throughout the house, the monochrome look is relieved with pops of sunny yellow that are here picked up in the flowers. The overall effect is relaxed and restful.

The property is in a conservation area, so we enlisted the help of local architect Charlotte Pither of Little House Design. Once planning permission was granted, local builder Andrew Fellas was hired to undertake the work. It was only possible to extend on the ground floor, due to planning limitations. A steel frame was inserted to support the back of the house, and two external walls were removed so that we could build out and create an open-plan kitchen-diner on the site of the existing back patio. A skylight over the extension allows light to flood into the new kitchen-diner, and the double-aspect windows from front to back mean the house is filled with daylight.

From the front of the house, the small red-brick cottage appears modest and unassuming, but now, upon walking through the front door, you are immediately drawn through the house to the back garden. The door between the sitting room and

RESTFUL RESTRAINT
Stoneware adds an earthy softness to an interior, and vintage linens create a laid-back aesthetic when combined with the warm tones of wood, natural slate and painted brick (*this page*). Keeping to a limited palette helps to maintain a calm and unfussy scheme, and adding natural elements such as stone and wood give texture and variety (*opposite*).

the kitchen was widened and supported with a steel joist, and the once-poky kitchen has been transformed into a generous kitchen-diner and a downstairs shower room with views out onto the garden and garden cabin beyond.

When it came to the decorating, my aim was to keep the house light and bright with a tranquil vibe, but I didn't want to go for a conventional coastal theme. Instead, I chose simple, pared-back wooden touches: painted floorboards, sisal flooring, painted brick and monochrome stripes. There's nothing self-consciously nautical, but rather tones and textures that are reminiscent of the windswept pebble beaches and weathered cabins typical of the area, and long winter walks along the coast.

In the kitchen, I chose a dark riven slate for the floor and the cabinets were handmade from leftover maple boards from our previous house. My husband Rich's father reclaimed the maple from an old Yorkshire dance floor many years back and we decided to use the remainder for the cabinets. As the kitchen isn't very big, this worked out perfectly. Rich sanded and cleaned every piece of wood, then our joiner Steve Buckley made the door fronts, which we fitted onto Howdens carcasses.

The sitting area was kept simple, with tongue and groove in the alcoves and painted brickwork on the chimney breast for additional texture. A Charnwood wood-burning stove was installed in the

RECLAIMED AND VINTAGE

Most of the furniture here is reclaimed or vintage bar the floor lamp from Design Vintage. An old armchair was given a new lease of life with a striped loose cover in Ian Mankin fabric, while the distressed shelf unit was picked up at a local antiques fair (*above*). The old IKEA sofa was an eBay purchase, and the blanket box that doubles as a coffee table was sourced from a local junk store (*opposite*).

fireplace, and the walls were painted a soft off-white to enhance the light. I have added lots of texture and character in the form of roughly painted floorboards, sisal rugs, linen upholstery and heaps of cushions on the banquette seating in the kitchen.

Upstairs, the build was a bit simpler. We took the space back to a shell and it was rewired and replumbed. The third bedroom, which was originally accessed from the second bedroom, was converted into an en-suite bathroom. The house didn't have an upstairs lavatory and we thought it important to have a bathroom upstairs. My intention was to keep the bedrooms quiet and restful, so the builders stripped the plaster off the fireplaces and took the walls back to the bare brick to add subtle textural interest. Little elements such as vintage seascapes, woven wicker shades, rustic furniture and painted peg rails ensure a relaxed vibe, with a slightly nostalgic nod to happy childhood holidays by the sea.

LIGHT AND BRIGHT

To keep the bedrooms as streamlined as possible, I hung peg rails all around the walls and fitted Roman blinds/shades in striped linen from Merchant & Mills. The furnishings and artworks are all vintage finds, teamed with lots of white to keep them fresh and calm (*this page*). Sisal flooring adds warmth and texture to the floor, and a large woven lampshade gives a focal point (*opposite*).

CALMING
COLOUR

Bold colours might not seem the obvious choice for a calm interior, but this elegant, reposeful Berkshire home dispels the myth that only pastel hues and off-whites can be tranquil and serene. The owners relocated from West London a few years ago, driven by a desire for country living. Their new home offered an upsize from their Victorian terrace, with more space for their growing family and brindle lurcher puppies, yet remains within commuter distance of the city.

'The part-Georgian, part-older, part-turn-of-the-century house has a pleasingly classical symmetrical exterior to the front and lots of fairly sympathetic additions and extensions made for a large but somehow cosy family house,' owner Clare Wilcox explains. With an easy layout, the ground-floor reception rooms flow together in a way that's very liveable. 'It's quite naturally open-plan for a period house, and you never feel like you're shut at one end of the house, far away from the rest of the action. Some elements feel grand and some cosy. I like the way these

COLOUR LOVERS

The entrance hall leads into the main dining space *(this page and opposite)*. Both rooms are painted in greens and blues that work beautifully together to provide a seamless visual flow between the two spaces. Pops of colour in the form of velvet chairs, vintage books, artworks and antique furnishings add interest but don't distract, cleverly complementing the main palette.

PLANT LIFE
Even the lighter spaces within the house boast generous pops of colour that add decorative interest. One of the internal doors at the back of the house is painted in an uplifting blue that sits beautifully against white walls and cottage-style doors (*above*). The tranquil green garden room, painted in Tracery by Little Greene, is filled with stripes and gentle patterns that are balanced by the abundance of plants to create a relaxing indoor oasis (*opposite*).

two different aspects of a period country house sit together, and the different personalities in the rooms. When we have friends over, we try to move between the different spaces, as they all have their own atmosphere,' Clare reflects.

When the family moved in during the summer of 2018, the interior was 'superficially quite smart' but slightly fusty and in need of a refresh. So they embarked on a full refurb. The house was large enough and the layout worked well, so there was no need to extend. 'We repurposed one of the spare bedrooms as a master bathroom, knocked down a couple of walls to open up the kitchen, replumbed, rewired and did a complete decorative overhaul,' Clare says. The plan was to introduce colour, pattern and a mix of old and new furniture to create 'something that felt younger, more vibrant and not very "country". We worked with Nicola Harding, who had helped out with one tricky room in our previous house – she was a neighbour and a friend of a friend, and the only person I considered working with. The brief has been entirely fulfilled with her help.'

When it came to colour, Nicola made her mark. 'She used lots of blues, greens and dusty pinks from Paint & Paper Library, Little Greene and Farrow & Ball. The schemes are bolder in some rooms and more restrained in others, but the colours all connect: the colour of the kitchen island repeats on the internal doors to the garden room and dining room. The colours may feel surprising, but they make sense as part of the whole, so none of it feels random.'

As a result, the flow throughout the house is calm and composed; nothing jars or jumps but gently glides from one space to the next. One of the most relaxing rooms is the snug. Now dark and cocooning, this is one of the only north-facing rooms and was originally incredibly cold. An external door was removed, and

STUDY SPACE
The family's need for relaxed yet uncluttered spaces where rooms are well-ordered but still characterful is very apparent in the study, where interesting vintage lighting, rich colour on the walls and pared-back decorative elements take centre stage (*this page and opposite*). The old wooden dining table that doubles as a desk, the sisal floorcovering and vintage kilim all work together to warm up the blue-green walls, making this a restful room that's conducive to concentration.

COLOUR SPLASH

This traditional country house has been transformed into something younger and vibrant thanks to a clever mix of colour, pattern and vintage and modern furniture. The cosy snug is calm and cocooning, with dark, sludgy green walls that give the room a sense of warm and comfort (*right*). Interesting and unexpected injections of colour bring the room to life: the rug, the picture, and vintage yellow table light. Clever design tricks such as the blue-painted skirting/baseboard and window frame mirror the blue in the coffee table, and all add up to a sense of order (*opposite*).

the walls and ceiling painted in Hornblende by Paint & Paper Library, a dark, sludgy green. The raspberry-coloured rug from Vanderhurd has a dense pile and the sofa is covered in a dark corduroy, adding to the luxurious effect. Clare admits, 'It's a room you have to tear yourself out of at the end of the night!'

Rooms have been carefully curated to keep the interior restful and clutter free. Clare has lots of old hardback books, sourced mainly from eBay, which add colour and interest. There is much artwork: combinations of old and new, affordable prints and vintage posters along with original contemporary pieces to sit and contemplate throughout. Lots of lamps and house plants help too. 'There's a lot of green in the house and the views

out to the garden. I think the green of house plants brought indoors adds to this and seems to work wherever you've put them,' says Clare. She adds, 'We are a family who enjoy a relaxed but uncluttered space. The rooms are full of interest, but well-ordered. [There are] cosy corners, with nice lighting and quirky bits and bobs, but without the detritus of everyday life.'

The carefully chosen wall lighting and lamps dotted at different heights around a room cast atmospheric shadows and create warmth and intimacy. In many of the rooms there is no overhead lighting, and spotlights have been kept to a minimum except where they are really needed. Clare confesses, 'I like incandescent bulbs when I can get them, so that the lamps cast a warmer light.'

PERFECTLY PATTERNED

The master bedroom is a masterclass in how to use pattern in an understated way. The headboard, cushions and rug all work together to add interest, but are tempered by the plain pastel hues on the walls, bedlinen, bedspread and bare floorboards (*this page*). The dressing room with built-in wardrobes/closets is sleek and unfussy, with only simple decorative elements such as the wicker chair and red lamp (*opposite*).

NATURE
STUDY

A GLIMPSE OF THE WATER
The living room floor is covered with terracotta pamments sliced from reclaimed 19th-century bricks from Eastern Europe, as well as a beautiful blue Märta Måås-Fjetterström rug (*above right*). The south wall features two large windows overlooking the River Alde, between which is a hearth wall faced with black steel that encompasses an open fire. Above the fireplace and window hangs a wall installation by ceramicist Valéria Nascimento (*opposite*).

As you enter the magnificent home of Ben Baglio and Richard Wilson in Suffolk, you are greeted with a vast window that draws your eye straight outside to the marshes and the wide expanse of the River Alde beyond. Built in 2015 and designed in conjunction with Mole Architects and Elaine Williams of Interior Couture, the house is wedge-shaped, with two storeys at one end and a low-ceilinged garden store at the other. All the main rooms were designed to face south towards the river, filling them with light all year round. The exterior is white-painted brick with the main structure made of timber. The sloping zinc roof extends from a sharp angle at the north end of the house to horizontal over the garden store.

'When we acquired the site, there was an existing marshkeeper's cottage from the 1930s that had been extended considerably in the 1970s. It was showing its age and was in a low-lying section of the property, in a flood plain,' Ben explains. 'We wanted a house that would maximize views over the marshes and allow lots of light to filter in. Very early on in the process, we discussed the number and sizes of rooms, how we like to live, our proposed budget and so on. Mole took this away and presented us with a choice of preliminary designs.

TREASURED COLLECTIONS
The living room furniture includes a mid-century walnut sideboard from Germany beneath a Serge Mouille three-armed light, and a pair of armchairs by Erik Jørgensen. The room is home to some of Ben and Richard's treasured collection of ceramics, including a trio of works by Hans Vangsø (*above*) and a collection of tower vases by Rupert Spira located on a shelf high above the room (*opposite*).

The wedge-shaped house that we ended up with was the most adventurous of them all.'

The couple also turned to interior designer Elaine Williams of Interior Couture early on in the process to help with the interiors – having worked with her before, they were confident that she would add value to the project. Ben and Richard wanted to use a limited range of materials in order to keep the space uniform and unfussy. 'Walls are either painted or panelled in oak and the floors are either oak or sections cut from reclaimed 19th-century bricks sourced from Eastern Europe. The floor in the kitchen is a customized terrazzo,' says Ben.

'The kitchen and dining area features a large pocket window that provides wonderful views and can be fully retracted in warm weather to give a feeling of being outdoors. The kitchen area has a large, granite-topped island that several people can gather round to prep and cook meals together,' Ben goes on.

The restricted colour palette is clean and restful. The kitchen, living room and hallway are all painted Iced Cube Silver by Benjamin Moore, a very pale blue-grey that changes character with the light. The ceiling in the foyer and the underside of the bulkhead in the living room are a very dark grey, Pitch Black by Farrow & Ball, which creates a sense of drama as the room opens up to its full height. The master bedroom suite is painted a calm warm mid-grey, which aids relaxation at the end of the day. The bedrooms all have high ceilings, but the oak-panelled walls behind the beds create a sense of cosiness.

However, there were two major challenges to overcome. 'The local council is open-minded

A PLACE FOR EVERYTHING
Considered placement of
furniture and accessories
is key to a calm and ordered
space; grouping objects
that go well together or are
in some way related helps
too. A gathering of elegant
Sara Moorhouse ceramics
on the bookshelves works
beautifully, injecting colour
and interest (*left*). Sleek
mid-century furniture brings
warmth, while soft grey walls
provide a serene backdrop
(*below and opposite*).

about contemporary architecture, but we
had to deal with numerous objections from
neighbours, the golf club, town council and a
district councillor, who argued that the house
would adversely affect tourism in the area!
Fortunately, the planning committee approved
the plans, there hasn't been a noticeable
decline in tourism and the fact that the house
went on to win several architectural awards
made us feel vindicated,' Ben smiles.

The second and more dramatic challenge
was the sudden flooding of Hazlewood
Marshes just before construction began in
December 2013. The highest tidal surge in
more than a century breached the earth wall
containing the tidal stretch of the river, and
brackish water flooded the bottom of the
garden twice a day. 'When it became clear
that the damaged river wall was not going
to be repaired, we decided to build our own
river defences to manage future issues,'

A PLACE TO EAT

The spacious kitchen centres on a large island with a honed dark grey granite top. On the wall is a black linen macrogauze wall hanging by Peter Collingwood (*above left*). The dining table is a reproduction Prouvé oak and painted metal model that seats eight on four vintage Hans Wegner Wishbone chairs and a custom-built blue-grey leather banquette designed by Elaine Williams (*opposite*). Ben and Richard worked with a lighting designer to find fittings to emphasize the tall ceilings and rafters in many of the rooms. In addition, they sourced several vintage and authentic reproduction light fittings to bring character to the interior spaces (*left and above right*).

explains Ben. 'This was a very large and unexpected expense. Happily, in the aftermath of the flood, a large area of reed bed sprang up on our land, and the new intertidal wetland provides us with alternating views of a greatly widened river and mudflats, which are a great draw for migrating birds and waders.'

Marsh Hill is a remarkably tranquil house, and an ideal place to relax. 'The view over the marshes, with the big constantly changing skies – there is always something to look at, the incoming tide, wildlife, clouds, spectacular sunsets,' says Ben. 'We feel we've succeeded in creating a restful, uncluttered interior. Above all, Marsh Hill is a place for us and our guests to unwind, and we aim to avoid visual "busyness" at all costs,' he concludes.

SOOTHING SLEEP SPACE

The master bedroom suite is painted in Papers and Paints SC377 Pure Grey 7, and the oak floors are covered with a Niki Jones Harlequin rug (*above right and opposite*). The room is furnished with a Matthew Hilton Hepburn bed (*above left*) and a Heal's Arts & Crafts chest (*page150*). Above the chest hangs a pen and wash drawing by Cavendish Morton of the interior of the nearby Snape Maltings concert hall during its conversion in 1967, one of Ben and Richard's favourite places.

A BATH WITH A VIEW
The guest bathroom is located between the
two guest bedrooms (*this page*). The green,
blue and white encaustic tiled floor is by Bert
& May, and the cream hexagonal wall tiles
are from Fired Earth. Custom cabinetry
designed by Elaine Williams is painted
dark blue, and pops of yellow in the
form of a striped Sara Moorhouse
bowl and a Zig Zag stool by
Pols Potten add brightness
to the room.

PERFECTLY COMPOSED

This was the last location that we had the pleasure of photographing for this book, and it didn't disappoint. In fact, it was a thrill to finish with this gem of a house in Gloucestershire. The wonderfully soulful and serene space is the result of a collaboration between the owners and Jodey Collorick, an interior designer and craftsman and the creative director of Kelmscott Studio based in nearby Stroud. 'I undertook the project management of the renovation of the cottage, advising, specifying and directing the refurbishment while trying to keep faithfully to my clients' vision, ethos and style,' Jodey explains.

The 17th-century stone cottage sits nestled on the edge of a pretty valley just outside Painswick in Gloucestershire. With multiple period details, the cottage even has an underground chamber built for secret cockfighting when it became outlawed, or so the locals say. It is located on the private Blow estate, which has Hilles House at its heart. Designed and built at the beginning of the last century by the prominent Arts & Crafts architect Detmar Blow, a friend and colleague of both William Morris and John

NATURAL STYLE
Interior designer Jodey Collorick's use of natural materials is at the heart of this home. 'I especially love reclaimed wood, with its character and imperfections,' he explains. Natural dyed linens, antique chairs – one covered in a patchwork of vintage fabric – vernacular furniture and bleached floorboards all contribute to the serene, muted palette (*this page and opposite*).

Ruskin, Hilles House has a long and interesting history of its own, with many colourful and creative characters passing through over the years.

The cottage has undergone a full refurbishment since the owners moved here at the end of 2020, but the layout has remained almost unchanged, apart from dividing the large living area with a partition wall to create a separate entrance hall-cum-dining space on the ground floor. Set over three storeys, with two bedrooms on the top floor and a beautiful bathroom overlooking the valley, two on the middle floor plus another bathroom, and the main living space downstairs, the interior is pared back and unfussy, with a muted colour palette enhanced by simple country furniture, natural dyed linens and lots of well-worn reclaimed textures and surfaces.

The entrance hall, painted in Paint & Paper Library's Slate IV, is flooded with light falling from a large window and has a built-in bench seat that was probably originally

THE GREAT DIVIDE

The downstairs living area has been divided into two. One half is now a snug, with an old stone fire surround as its main feature; the walls are painted mid-grey and there are lots of natural textures in the form of wood, wool and linens (*opposite and above right*). The other half is now a dining room-cum-hall, where the walls have been panelled to add interest (*above left*).

TIMELESS APPEAL
The dining hall has a quiet, contemplative quality. It is an uncluttered space and the interest here lies in the graceful curve of the staircase, the old wooden table and benches, the newly panelled walls, original leaded windows and wooden floorboards (*this page and opposite*).

COUNTRY KITCHEN
The simple kitchen is considered and functional. A wooden rack above the reclaimed double sink acts as a shelf-cum-draining board. Old chopping /cutting boards are housed in the fireplace, cleaning equipment is hidden behind a vintage linen curtain and a sturdy old wooden table doubles as a central island and dining table.

used for weaving, as this area was known for its cottage industries connected to the cloth trade. The kitchen, with its uneven white plaster walls, is made up of reclaimed cabinets matched with new joinery that was sensitively designed to look as if it had always been there.

'The clients had a clear vision of the style direction from the outset, and everything flowed from this', Jodey says. 'It turned out that the clients' previous house was one of my favourite interiors, so I knew straight away that we would work well stylistically together.'

The owners had already decided on the colours they wanted to use in their new home, opting for gentle, restful shades – nothing too dominant or attention-grabbing. 'Most of the house is painted in James White by Farrow & Ball. We specified all of the paint finishes to be as matt as possible, using [Farrow & Ball specialist finishes] Casein Distemper on the walls and Dead Flat for the woodwork,' Jodey explains. These matt finishes still and calm the light by absorbing any reflections – it's a subtle but important detail that contributes to the peaceful feel. The floorboards were bleached with lye soap to soften the wood tones.

'It can be a challenge when working with so many reclaimed materials and fittings. Sourcing the right things in the right sizes can be time-consuming, wood can be warped and need straightening out or an old sink and tap/faucets might

CUPBOARD LOVE

A newly built cabinet houses the refrigerator and is painted a creamy muted tone to match the lime-plastered walls and stonework. Investing in lots of table lamps and avoiding ceiling spotlights will create a space that feels both intimate and atmospheric. A classic column radiator from B&Q is in keeping with the style of the house while pumping out plenty of 21st-century warmth (*above*).

not marry up with modern bathroom fittings, for example, but when it works, it guarantees a home that is truly soulful, full of earthy serenity and warmth,' Jodey remarks.

The house certainly feels homely and welcoming, filled with treasured pieces of furniture and other objects collected over the years by the owners. It also feels extremely calm and composed. 'I try to use neutral, earthy colour schemes, allowing an easy flow as you move from room to room, and limewash or distemper for a matt chalky feel. I like to use things from the past; they have a soulful character. Strip things back, don't have more than you need, only have things that you love,' says Jodey. This simple yet considered decorating philosophy cannot help but create a soothing and tranquil home.

SLEEP EASY

In the small bathroom, old planks fitted horizontally have been painted to lighten the space and, along with the uncurtained window, give a sense of calm (*above left*). The spare bedroom, with a wooden bed base that sits neatly in the eaves, is clutter free, save for a lamp with a woven shade that adds interest and texture (*above right*). The main bedroom is simply furnished, with pops of colour coming from the artworks that are propped up casually along one wall (*opposite*).

RELAXED
LIVING

Nestled quietly among the bustling streets of
St Ives, you'd be forgiven for walking straight past
this little oasis of a cottage. The owners, Paula and
Iain Craigen, have managed to create a retreat
that is the epitome of relaxed living, where deep,
squashy linen sofas, rustic wooden furniture,
bare floorboards, tonal fabrics and whitewashed
walls all come together to create a bright yet calm
interior. There's nothing here that clamours for
attention. Instead, the simplicity of the interior
allows your eye to glide from one side of the
room to the other with restful ease.

Built from granite and cob, the house was
once three fishermen's cottages with a pink-
painted facade. 'The Pink House', as it's
affectionately known by locals, is a prominent
feature of Porthmeor Beach in St Ives, Cornwall.

'Around 1840, a Mr Edward Harry had an old bakehouse demolished to build 10 fishermen's cottages set around a central courtyard. The house remained in the same ownership for more than 60 years until we bought it,' explains Paula Craigen.

The layout has been kept intrinsically as it was, but Paula and Iain removed a wall between the kitchen and sitting room to ensure that there was a sea view from (almost) every room in the house. 'We designed the interiors alongside Jess Clark from Unique Homestays, working with the bones of the original cottages,' says Paula. 'We retained as much of the character and charm as possible, embracing the old floorboards, sloping walls and irregular alcoves. We further enhanced the rustic feel with reclaimed finds and furniture to give the property an eclectic artist's studio edge.'

The Craigens painted the interior chalky white throughout, then added natural hues, lots of linen and accents of chalky green inspired by the dining-room

PEACEFUL HAVEN

The house is a little oasis hidden among the busy streets of St Ives, Cornwall. Paula and Iain kept as many of the original features of the cottage as possible, including the beams, floorboards and fitted cabinetry. To this, they added mix-and-match antique and vintage furniture, interesting reclaimed bits and pieces and utility-style lighting. A palette of pale neutrals keeps the mood tranquil and relaxed, as do the two deep, squashy Howard-style linen sofas (*pages 162–163, this page and opposite*).

floorboards. But really this cottage is all about the setting. 'We wanted guests to be immersed in the ever-changing seascape of Porthmeor Beach, without a scheme that was shouting for their attention inside. The rooms are light-filled and calming, with lots of interesting objects,' says Paula. Much of the furniture was sourced from reclamation yards, and these pieces are mixed with vintage nauticalia that's rich in patina and texture.

'It was a full renovation,' Paula explains. 'My husband carried out the majority of the work over a six-month period. We restored the original sash windows, sanded the floorboards, built a bespoke kitchen from reclaimed wood, replumbed and rewired and created an open-plan feel through from the kitchen to ensure that pretty much every room made the most of the views. We added a downstairs toilet and created a Jack and Jill bathroom in addition to the family bathroom upstairs. We also installed a bathtub in one of the bedrooms, from which the most amazing sunsets can be enjoyed. Iain dedicated six months to the renovation and personally crafted many of the elements that make the house unique. Throughout the property, we feature art created by a close friend of ours that is inspired by St Ives.'

Paula says the house makes her feel 'as if I've escaped the everyday. There's little downtime when we're at home, with a large family and busy work lives. When we are here, we have the chance to properly take a breath and relax. I can sit for hours watching the water. The sunsets are amazing and storm watching even more so. And I'll never tire of falling asleep to the sound of the sea. It's a sociable

house too, and I like the informality of the spaces that we've created. It's such a comfortable, liveable space; ideal for family time after a day at the beach.'

Each room has a window seat for wave watching, while the tonal colour scheme brings a tranquil feel to the spaces. 'When we stay in the winter, there's a cosy feeling inside – we light the wood burner and listen to the waves roaring,' Paula explains. 'The neutral decor combined with soft lighting and the ever-changing view is very relaxing. It's a retreat from our everyday lives that allows us to spend quality time together.'

BRINGING ORDER

'Every single item should be there for a reason: the books that you choose, the crockery that you feature,' says Paula. The kitchen, which was made from repurposed wood, feels as if it's always been there. Ceramics and kitchen accessories from Nkuku and Kitchenalia are stacked neatly onto open shelves – a place for everything, and everything in its place (*opposite and above*).

WHITE AND BRIGHT

The interior has been whitewashed from top to bottom, allowing all the natural elements to sing out from a clean white canvas. The main bathroom is simple, with a few contrasting touches in the form of artwork, mirrors and accessories (*above*). The bedrooms, too, are understated, with wooden shutters, neutral bedlinen, a scattering of interesting artworks and industrial-style lighting (*above right and right*).

SOAK AND SLEEP

The house is filled with appealing textures – bare, scuffed floorboards, wooden beams and intriguing nooks and crannies. In one of the bedrooms, the linen bedding is from Piglet in Bed and the wooden bedside cabinet and woven Lloyd Loom-style chair are vintage, while framed seaweed prints give a nod to the house's coastal location.

SOURCE BOOK

PAINTS AND FABRICS

Atelier Ellis
atelierellis.co.uk
Beautiful water-based
environmentally friendly
paint that dries to a
wonderful flat finish.

Bauwerk Colour
bauwerkcolour.co.uk
Environmentally friendly
lime paints made with clay,
minerals and natural
pigments.

Clayworks Plaster
clay-works.com
Natural clay plasters that
are healthy and breathable
for walls and ceilings.

The Cloth Shop
theclothshop.net
New and vintage fabrics
and accessories. A real
treasure-trove that I love.

Edward Bulmer
edwardbulmerpaint.co.uk
Natural paints in earthy
textural colours and
pigments with a finish you
want to touch.

Ian Mankin
ianmankin.co.uk
My go-to for stripes and
ticking fabrics.

Kathryn Davey
Kathryndavey.com
Sustainable design studio
specializing in naturally
dyed homewares plus
natural dye kits.

Linen Me
linenme.com
Simple linens in a variety
of colours and designs.

Little Greene
Littlegreene.com
Environmentally friendly
paints for interior and
exteriors in a huge range
of gorgeous colours that
I use in lots of projects.

Merchant & Mills
merchantandmills.com
Unique and beautiful
fabric, buttons and trims
in a wonderful array of
colours and textures.

Parna Ltd
Parna.co.uk
Online stockist of vintage
linens, cushion covers and
grain sacks.

Vanessa Arbuthnott Fabrics
vanessaarbuthnott.co.uk
Organic linens inspired by
the flora and fauna of the
English countryside.

Volga Linen
volgalinen.com
Linens for the bedroom,
table and bathroom as
well as fabric by the metre.

ACCESSORIES AND FURNITURE

Aerende
aerende.co.uk
Lovingly sourced
collections of handmade
items for your home.

Among the Pines
amongthepines.gallery
Online art gallery featuring
affordable originals by a
selection of artists.

Baileys Home
baileyshome.com
Destination home store
housed in a series of old
farm buildings near
Ross-on-Wye.

Caravane
caravane.fr
Furniture, fabrics, lighting,
rugs and beautiful linens
from France.

Dante Ceramics
dantesceramics.com
Handmade stoneware for
slow living.

Fabulous Vintage Finds
fabulousvintagefinds.co.uk
A wonderful source of
reclaimed and vintage
finds, accessories and
lighting for the home.

Harp Studio
harp-studio.com
Calm, considered
accessories for a pared-
back minimalist home.

Labour and Wait
labourandwait.co.uk
Functional and simple
hardware, clothing and
accessories.

Larusi
larusi.com
Renowned for tribal rugs
and textiles from Morocco.

Lucy Rutter
lucyrutter.com
A ceramicist inspired by
the landscape of the Kent
marshes.

Maison Artefact
maisonartefact.com
Beautiful simple, and
elegant antiques found
by Vicky Davar, who will
also source for you.

Pottery West
potterywest.co.uk
Hand thrown and hand
glazed stoneware lovingly
made in Sheffield UK.

Robert Young Antiques
robertyoungantiques.com
A great selection of
primitive antique furniture.

Tinsmiths
tinsmiths.co.uk
A veritable treasure-trove
for fabrics, lighting and
homewares that feature
a lot in my own home.

Will and Bea
willandbea.co.uk
Antiques and homeware
that will inspire simple
everyday living.

FLOORING
Alternative Flooring
alternativeflooring.com
Carpets, runner and rugs
in different designs and
styles, whatever your taste.

Bert and May
bertandmay.com
A wonderful selection of
new and reclaimed tiles,
often in limited stocks and
colours for a unique home.

Crucial Trading
crucial-trading.com
Wool, sisal, sisool, coir,
seagrass and jute flooring
that will bring the beauty
of nature inside.

Dinesen
dinesen.com
High-quality engineered
and solid wooden planks
for floors, panelling,
cladding and ceilings.

Mandarin Stone
mandarinstone.com
Natural and stone flooring
in a huge variety of
finishes from slate to
marble, plus porcelain
and ceramic tiles.

Tate and Darby
tateanddarby.com
Vintage and handmade
kilims, Beni Ourain rugs
and sisal floor coverings.

Woca
wocadenmark.co.uk
Environmentally friendly
wood care solutions for
treating, maintaining and
cleaning wood. I use this
on my floorboards to
whiten and treat them.

PICTURE CREDITS

Front endpaper: Josephine Ryan Antiques in Tetbury, josephineryanantiques.myshopify.com; 1 Designed by Jodey Collorick of Kelmscottstudio.co.uk; 2–3 The London home of Elise Ovanessoff and Stephen Quinn of WORKS Architecture; 4 Designed by Jodey Collorick of Kelmscottstudio.co.uk; 5–6 The London home of Elise Ovanessoff and Stephen Quinn of WORKS Architecture; 7 The home of Ben Baglio and Richard Wilson in Suffolk, www.benbaglio.com; 8–9 House available to rent via @blackshorestay and sallydenning.com; 10 centre Josephine Ryan Antiques in Tetbury, josephineryanantiques. myshopify.com; 12 Alba Beach House, Cornwall, available to rent through Unique Homestays, uniquehomestays.com; 13 above Alba Beach House, Cornwall, available to rent through Unique Homestays uniquehomestays.com; 13 below The Cheshire home of architect and interior designer Annabelle Tugby, www.annabelletugbyarchitects.co.uk; 14 Interior design by Nicola Harding & Co.;15 left Josephine Ryan Antiques in Tetbury, josephineryanantiques.myshopify.com; 15 right Designed by Jodey Collorick of Kelmscottstudio.co.uk; 17 Interior design and antiques by Victoria Davar of Maison Artefact; 19 left The London home of Elise Ovanessoff and Stephen Quinn of WORKS Architecture; 20 left Designed by Jodey Collorick of Kelmscottstudio.co.uk; 20 centre Designed by Jodey Collorick of Kelmscottstudio.co.uk; 20 right Ukiyo, Cornwall available to rent through Unique Homestays, uniquehomestays.com; 21 The Cheshire home of architect and interior designer Annabelle Tugby, www.annabelletugbyarchitects.co.uk; 22 Coastal House, Devon, 6a architects; 23 Ukiyo, Cornwall available to rent through Unique Homestays uniquehomestays.com; 25 The home of Ben Baglio and Richard Wilson in Suffolk www.benbaglio.com; 26 Interior design and antiques by Victoria Davar of Maison Artefact; 27 The home of Ben Baglio and Richard Wilson in Suffolk www.benbaglio.com; 28 above Designed by Jodey Collorick of Kelmscottstudio.co.uk; 28 below left Interior design and antiques by Victoria Davar of Maison Artefact; 28 below right Designed by Jodey Collorick of Kelmscottstudio.co.uk; 29 House available to rent via @blackshorestay and sallydenning.com; 30 Josephine Ryan Antiques in Tetbury, josephineryanantiques.myshopify.com; 32 left Designed by Jodey Collorick of Kelmscottstudio.co.uk; 32 centre Designed by Jodey Collorick of Kelmscottstudio.co.uk; 32 right Coastal House, Devon, 6a architects; 33 The London home of Elise Ovanessoff and Stephen Quinn of WORKS Architecture; 34 Designed by Jodey Collorick of Kelmscottstudio.co.uk; 35 Interior design by Nicola Harding & Co.; 36 left House available to rent via @blackshorestay and sallydenning.com; 36 centre The Cheshire home of architect and interior designer Annabelle Tugby, www.annabelletugbyarchitects.co.uk; 36 right Interior design and antiques by Victoria Davar of Maison Artefact; 37 Ukiyo, Cornwall available to rent through Unique Homestays, uniquehomestays.com; 38 Alba Beach House, Cornwall, available to rent through Unique Homestays, uniquehomestays.com; 39 above left Alba Beach House, Cornwall, available to rent through Unique Homestays, uniquehomestays.com; 39 right Interior design and antiques by Victoria Davar of Maison Artefact; 39 below left The London home of Elise Ovanessoff and Stephen Quinn of WORKS Architecture; 40 The Cheshire home of architect and interior designer Annabelle Tugby, www.annabelletugbyarchitects.co.uk; 41 left The Cheshire home of architect and interior designer Annabelle Tugby, www.annabelletugbyarchitects.co.uk; 41 right The home of Ben Baglio and Richard Wilson in Suffolk, www.benbaglio.com; 42 above left The Cheshire home of architect and interior designer Annabelle Tugby, www.annabelletugbyarchitects.co.uk; 42 above right Josephine Ryan Antiques in Tetbury, josephineryanantiques. myshopify.com; 42 below left The London home of Elise Ovanessoff and Stephen Quinn of WORKS Architecture; 42 above right Alba Beach House, Cornwall, available to rent through Unique Homestays, uniquehomestays.com; 43 The London home of Elise Ovanessoff and Stephen Quinn of WORKS Architecture; 44–45 Designed by Jodey Collorick of Kelmscottstudio.co.uk; 46–57 Josephine Ryan Antiques in Tetbury, josephineryanantiques. myshopify.com; 58–67 Ukiyo, Cornwall available to rent through Unique Homestays, uniquehomestays.com; 68–77 Coastal House Devon, 6a architects; 78–87 The London home of Elise Ovanessoff and Stephen Quinn of WORKS Architecture; 88–97 The Cheshire home of architect and interior designer Annabelle Tugby, www.annabelletugbyarchitects.co.uk; 110–119 Interior design and antiques by Victoria Davar of Maison Artefact; 120–129 House available to rent via @blackshorestay and sallydenning.com; 130–139 Interior design by Nicola Harding & Co.;140–151 The home of Ben Baglio and Richard Wilson in Suffolk www.benbaglio.com; 152–161 Designed by Jodey Collorick of Kelmscottstudio.co.uk; 162–169 Alba Beach House, Cornwall, available to rent through Unique Homestays uniquehomestays.com; 171 Coastal House, Devon, 6a architects; 173 The home of Ben Baglio and Richard Wilson in Suffolk www.benbaglio.com; 176 The home of Ben Baglio and Richard Wilson in Suffolk www.benbaglio.com; back endpaper: The home of Ben Baglio and Richard Wilson in Suffolk www.benbaglio.com.

BUSINESS CREDITS

6a architects
Rapier House
40 Lambs Conduit Street
London WC1N 3LJ
+ 44 (0)20 7242 5422
post@6a.co.uk
6a.co.uk
Pages 22; 32 right; 68–77;
171.

Alba Beach House
Unique Homestays
+ 44 (0)1637 355863
uniquehomestays.com
Pages 12; 13 above; 38;
39 above left; 42 above
right; 162–169.

Annabelle Tugby
Architects
The Workshop
Norcliffe Estate
Styal
Cheshire SK9 4LH
Pages 13 below; 21; 36
centre; 40; 41 left; 42
above left; 88–97.

Ben Baglio
benbaglio.com
Architect
Mole Architects
Floor 2, Burleigh House
52 Burleigh Street
Cambridge CB1 1DJ
studio@molearchitects.
co.uk
+ 44 (0)1223 913012
molearchitect.co.uk
and

Interior Couture
studio@interiorcouture.
com
+ 44 (0)20 3664 1022
interiorcouture.com
Available to hire through:
Peagreen Locations
The Courtyard
Heath Farm
Brickyard Hill
Garsdon
Malmesbury
Wiltshire SN16 9NW
info@peagreenlocations.
com
+ 44 (0)1666 539549
peagreenlocations.com
Pages 7; 25; 27; 41 right;
140–151; 173; 176.

Jodey Collorick
Kelmscott Studio
104 Bath Road
Stroud
Gloucestershire GL5 3TJ
+ 44 (0)7904 354299
kelmscottstudio.co.uk
Pages 1; 4; 15 right; 20
left; 20 centre; 28 above;
28 below right; 32 left;
32 centre; 34; 44–45;
152–161.

Josephine Ryan Antiques
44 Long Street
Tetbury
Gloucestershire GL8 8AQ
jryantiques@aol.com
+ 44 (0)7973 336 149
josephineryanantiques.
myshopify.com
Pages 10 centre; 15 left;
30; 42 above; 46–47.

Victoria Davar
Maison Artefact
273 Lillie Road
Fulham
London SW6 7LL
+ 44 (0)20 73812500
mail@maisonartefact.com
and
Architect & design studio
Edenkido
Richard@edenkido.com
edenkido.com
Pages 17; 26; 28 below
left; 36 right; 39 right;
110–119.

Nicola Harding & Co.
31 Lonsdale Road
London NW6 6RA
+ 44 (0)20 8743 6690
hello@nicolaharding.com
nicolaharding.com
Pages 14; 35; 130–135.

Sally Denning
studio@sallydenning.com
sallydenning.com
builder
Andrew Fellas
andrwefellas1975@yahoo.
co.uk
+ 44 (0)7786 733693
architectural services
Charlotte Pither
Little House Design
+ 44 (0)7962 005779
Pages 8–9; 29; 36 left;
120–139.

Ukiyo, Cornwall
Unique Homestays
+ 44 (0)1637 355863
uniquehomestays.com
Interior design by
Kathryn Tyler
Linea Studio
ktyler@linea-studio.co.uk
+ 44 (0)7973 639931
linea-studio.co.uk
Pages 20 right; 23; 37;
58–67.

WORKS Architecture Ltd
16 Upper Montagu Street
London W1H 2AN
mail@worksarchitecture.
com
+ 44 (0)20 7224 8750
worksarchitecture.com
Pages 2–3; 5–6; 19 left;
33; 39 below left; 42 below
left; 43; 78–87.

INDEX

Page numbers in italic refer to the illustrations

THANK YOU

Planning, organising, photographing, shooting, styling, art directing and writing a book during a global pandemic has been a challenge, to say the least, but we got there (just!). I would like to thank everyone at RPS who helped make my idea come to life. Thank you to Cindy, for believing in this project. Organizing all the location photography is the most mammoth real-life jigsaw puzzle, for which I am eternally grateful to Jess at RPS. Thank you Jess for your help, for being a sounding board and for your sense of humour when everything was going wrong. Thank you also to Annabel, whose patience and support has meant a great deal pre-, during and post-lockdowns, and for gently nagging me for words when she needed them, and to Megan, who understood my creative brain and designed a book that looks cohesive and beautiful.

Thank you also to all the location owners. After 25 years as a stylist, I know that it's an honour and privilege to be welcomed into someone's home: their retreat, their safe space. I hope that Polly and I have done your homes justice and shown them off at their absolute best. Thank you for opening your doors to us.

Thank you to my family, as always: my incredible husband, who supports my work 100% even when the juggle is above and beyond; my boys, who are my absolute world; and Buster, our dog, who has brought more happiness than I could ever have imagined.

Lastly, thank you to Polly, the most inspiring and wonderful photographer I know. To be able to work with, laugh with and cry with you has been, and will always be, an absolute joy, and I am so thankful you agreed to do this project with me. Thank you for everything – for helping me see things differently and the bread for lunch xxx